Feelings

For those who have laughed and cried... with others and alone

Written by: Lawrence Brenner | Illustrations by: Elwyn Mehlman

Archway Publishing books may be ordered through booksellers or by contacting:

Archway Publishing
1663 Liberty Drive
Bloomington, IN 47403
www.archwaypublishing.com
844-669-3957

Because of the dynamic nature of the Internet, any web addresses or links contained in this book may have changed since publication and may no longer be valid. The views expressed in this work are solely those of the author and do not necessarily reflect the views of the publisher, and the publisher hereby disclaims any responsibility for them.

Any people depicted in stock imagery provided by Getty Images are models, and such images are being used for illustrative purposes only.
Certain stock imagery © Getty Images.

ISBN: 978-1-6657-0086-3 (sc)
ISBN: 978-1-6657-0087-0 (hc)
ISBN: 978-1-6657-0088-7 (e)

Library of Congress Control Number: 2020925492

Print information available on the last page.

Archway Publishing rev. date: 12/30/2020

Feelings

A walk through good times
And not so good times

Cry Softly!
Laugh Loudly!
Enjoy!

Written by: Lawrence Brenner
Illustrated by: Elwyn Mehlman

Mom and Dad
Wish you were here!

―――――――――――

Marilee
my wife, my love, my best friend
who's fingers still hurt from typing pages...
over and over and over!

―――――――――――

Oops!! The Family
David, Jeffrey, Ellen, Amanda,
Colin, Tommy and Patrick

―――――――――――

Elwyn, with your brillant graphics, you gave life to my
writing and humor. Partner... You're the best!

And finally, to everyone I forgot to mention.

As long as we can remember Happy Beginnings
And dream of Happy Endings
We can handle the in-between

Everyone…young and old
Running…reaching for their goal
Listening for that final cheer
A cheer that they will never hear

They once laughed and cried
With others and alone
We'll always remember those
Who won't be coming home

We come back
We survive
We're alive today
All for one and one for all

It's the American Way
Run Boston Run
Run America Run

It's what we stand for
It's what we run for

You're not scaring us away
We're not going anywhere today
If there's a way – we will find
Our way to that finish line

It's the American Way
Run Boston Run
Run America Run

It's the American Way

J

Just wanted to let you know
There's someone special in my life
And I wanted you to know
He asked me to be his wife

I wish you were here
To share how I feel
Tell this little girl of yours
That this love is for real

I wish you were here
To help pick out my dress
Fix my hair and my makeup
After my making a mess

You told me I'd know
When I looked in his eyes
If I saw Daddy's smile
And felt our temperature rise

I wish you were here
To watch Daddy give me away
Instead of resting here
And never taken away

I wish you were here
To fix all those things
That wait for me
With the changes life brings

I wish you were here
Walking away with me
Holding my hand
For the world to see

Hey Mom!
I wish you were here

"What if" a boy like me
Can be with this beautiful girl I see
"What if" this boy wasn't young anymore
And was the one she was waiting for

"What if" she feels what I feel inside
That feeling I am trying to hide
"What if" whatever I long to dream
Maybe comes true for this here teen

Living with "What if"
Is a dream I can live with
A dream I can live with today

"What if" my future could see
Hundreds of photos with her and me
"What if" love now, may seem like never
Might turn out to be forever

"What if" we'd just been born today
Differences thrown away
"What if" I wish all my "What ifs" to be
Just with this beautiful girl I see

Living with "What if"
Is a dream I can live with
A dream I can live with today

A dream I can live with today

Me…just a kid
Interviewing a star
Right here, right now
It feels so bizzare

But she's real, not a dream
This moment's so extreme
Isn't it crazy, isn't it rich
A star with me, what a switch

She's awesome, she's funny
Anyone's reason to live
I'd give all my money
If I had any to give

I can ask her questions all day
And into the night
To keep her right here
While I smile and write

Isn't it crazy, isn't it rich
A star with me, what a stitch

The questions I ask
Should be of a scholarly tone
Not shrill sounding
Or monotone

Not invasive, not tacky
Just middle of the road
Stick to exactly
What I've been taught and been told

It's just an interview, after all
And no matter how hard I try
She'll answer my last question
And then say goodbye

To me
Isn't that a stitch

T HE MORE TIME I SPEND WITH YOU
THE MORE MEMORIES I HAVE
TO KEEP ME COMPANY
WHEN MEMORIES ARE ALL I HAVE

We were just born today

Differences thrown away

No reaching for my hand
To help build castles in the sand
Not feeling your sweet lips on mine
And wanting to freeze us in time

Nothing here feels the same
Without you calling out my name
I can't believe you're leaving me
With just pictures of what used to be

Painful complicated days
Unlike easy simple ways
When love was new
For me-For you

Yes!
Nothing here feels the same
As I watch our once burning flame
Flicker, dance and fade
With promises that we made

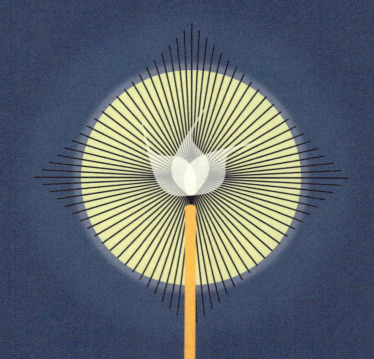

A dime is all he asked for

Yet, I turned away.

And so did he

As if he knew

I was refused today.

Yes, I saw a blind man.

I saw him look at me.

W

e're students
Moon dreamers
Tomorrow's gleamers

We're singers
We're dancers
We're movie enhancers

Composers
Musicians
Lighting Technicians

Dreamers like you
Dreamers like me
Bring entertainment for the world to see

We're gofers
We're scrappers
Anything but nappers

We're Shakespeare
And Vaudeville
Our names on the Playbill

We're listening
We're learning
Minds bursting with yearning

Dreamers like you
Dreamers like me
Bring entertainment for the world to see

We're producers
Sound mixers
And costume fixers

We're stuntmen
We're models
Future screen idols

Dreamers like you
Dreamers like me
Bring entertainment for the world to see

We're directors
Reciters
Drama screen writers

We're artists
Designers
Future headliners

We're trumpets
Guitarists
Recording artists

Just one page away
From the stage
And Broadway

Dreamers like you
Dreamers like me

I remember my first Valentine
And those words "Will you be mine"
Only dreams and wishes then
When grownup things were just pretend

Now each day is just like paradise
And each day with you I realize
All those dreams I've yet to find
Will come true if you'll be mine

Will you be my Valentine
Share your heart with me
Will you be my Valentine
Ev-ryday now, for eternity

And if anyone should ever ask
Tell them all you were my first and last
Valentine I always knew
That my heart was meant for you

Grew up in boots
Guitar strings strumm'n in my head
Remembering my roots
And true country hang'n by a thread

No more country music
Without meaning for me
Not till words tell the story
How country used to be

I'M TRADING COUNTRY FOR COUNTRY
THE WAY IT USED TO BE
I'M WAIST DEEP IN LOVE WITH COUNTRY
THE WAY COUNTRY USED TO BE

Buy'n a ticket
For I don't know where
Somewhere words and music
Tell a story I can share

With those who laughed and cried
With others and alone
And letting me inside
To bring true country home

Words that give
A story that lives
That's what I'm search'n for
For country-when country was more

I'M TRADING COUNTRY FOR COUNTRY
THE WAY IT USED TO BE
I'M WAIST DEEP IN LOVE WITH COUNTRY
THE WAY IT USED TO BE

For me

Loneliness is an icicle melting
My bicycle walking me home
My very first date
When all I did was wait alone

Loneliness is biting my lip
And swallowing a tear
Going steady when I wasn't ready to
Seeing her walk home with someone new

Loneliness is getting engaged
Thinking I'm past the age for spring
Walking that aisle
When all the while wondering

Loneliness is having a wife
Giving her life and more to you
And telling her you found
Found somebody new

Loneliness is biting my lip
Swallowing a tear
And wondering what to do

The crowd that surrounded us seemed miles away

I don't remember
Her taking her arms from around me

Just her half smiling face
Glancing from the half frosted window
Of the moving bus

I inhaled the last of the bus's fumes

I waved goodbye
To the sweet smelling memories of spring

But then!
Spring comes every year.

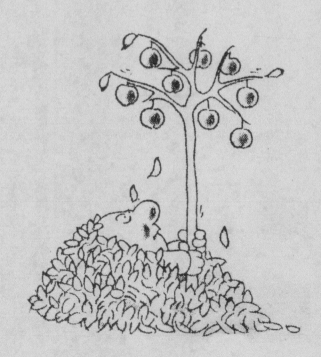

I'd like to write about
This love I have for you
But everything's been said before
There's nothing that is new

I could write of sadness
Of birds that never sing
It's been said so many different ways
And just what did it bring

How can I say something
That's been said before
How can I say nothing
When I mean more

Where can I find those words
I want so very much to say
Words you haven't heard
Day after day

I could write of heartaches
Use all those old clichés
Say anything and everything
Just to help me pass the days

I know you've heard it all
A million times or more
But I'll try and try again
A million times or more

When our eyes first met

You blushed away

Like a pale rose, I recall.

We held hands that first day

And as young as we were,

Our love was not as small.

I wish I was younger. As young as when,

The sun was much brighter and warmer than today.

And you were alive and full as a flower,

It's no wonder He chose you that day.

People look at me funny,

When I laugh aloud with you.

Me- Holding hands with a sentimental view.

I can't feel the cold, or see the bareness of fall,

Just warmth surrounding the prettiest flower of all.

Yes, I wish I was younger. As young as when

Others could see you the way I do today,

Alive as a breeze, kissed by falling leaves.

It's no wonder He chose you that day.

I'll always remember you that way.

Hello! I'm here
Is this really me in the mirror?
Who are you?

Always running, running, running
Afraid to stay
Seeing ev-rything from far away
Who are you – anyway?

Hello mirror

Are you seeing ev-ryone who passes thru my life
Thru rose colored glasses
When they aren't really in my life

Are you looking back at me and seeing anyone
Or just someone being caught
Trying to get home
Between me and everyone

Who are you anyway
Who are you anyway
Always running, running, running

Afraid to stay
Seeing ev-rything from far away
Who are you anyway

Maybe going home is what I needed all along
And change ev-rything that's going wrong

Goodbye mirror!

We'll remember home
Family that we love
And dreams we're still dreaming of

We'll remember home
And those we left behind
Reaching out for better times

We'll remember home
Land worth fighting for
So our children will have more
More than just another War

One day we'll come home
To the freedom that we know
Where we'll all hold hands
And never let go

Meanwhile

In our hearts we'll carry with us
Pictures of our home that once was
It's just what a soldier does

Till we're home again

Maybe someday,
They'll come true for me
Those fairy tales you told
When I sat upon your knee

Maybe someday,
The clouds will disappear
And let the sun shine in
And dry each and every tear

Maybe someday,
You'll sing that lullaby
With the happiest of endings,
Where no one ever says good-bye

Where are all those dreams you promised
Will those wishes all come true
Let me sit upon your knee
And wish one more time with you

Maybe someday,
That little girl in me,
Will look into a mirror again
And see her smiling back at me

Maybe someday,
I'll awake and find,
Someone calling out my name,
While I'm still on his mind

Maybe someday,
I'll look up and find
Everything I've looked for,
Was right here all the time

Daddy, all those dreams you promised
And wishes will come true
If I sit upon your knee
And wish one more time with you

Nothing's changed since then
All we lost was time
Remember how it was
When we shared our space in time

We were young and free
Wondering where to go
Wanting just to flee
Wanting just to know

Was there any reason or rhyme
In looking for our season and time
When I loved you
And you loved me all this time

I think of you each day
Your smile was everywhere
I could almost feel
Your touch in the air

Was there any reason or rhyme
In looking for our season and time
When I loved you
And you loved me all this time

Often I'd say my prayers
To those ducks lined in white
When thoughts of you
Would wake me at night.

Remembering when we smiled
At their giving one a shove
Those funny things holding wings
As if they were in love.

Wading white-procession like
This day
Quiet, fluttering not.
As if they knew our way.

T

They would circle me and laugh
Kids tearing me in half
I wanted just to hide me

They never took a second look
Beyond the cover of this book
To see what was inside me

I was made to feel less
And not fit in with the rest
They tried every way to break me

But, in my heart I was more
In my mind I could soar
Wherever dreams would take me

Now they circle me and laugh
They are my better half
I know they're laughing with me

Now they take me as I am
That's why I am better than
The dreams that helped to make me

I know my voice will last
Beyond my problem past
And know they hear what I say

There were times I cast a stone
Causing me to feel alone
But I'm not alone on this day

They were my eyes
Through the times I couldn't find me
Opening the skies
For the wind behind me
To find me

N
ow I guess it ends,
Or is it the beginning?
When one pretends,
Is it losing or is it winning?

Now when we meet,
It's the other way around.
Your feet – not mine
Firmly on the ground.

Maybe it wasn't you,
Or me,
Maybe just children being young,
Being who they'd like to be,
Then sticking out their tongue.

Best I forget your name
And hollow thoughts that fill your eyes,
Maybe it was just a game,
Children loving in disguise.

Will you spend the rest of your life with me.
Dream your dreams
Follow the sun with me.
Show the world our rainbow carrying us
Over the clouds
With the whole world daring us

Singing, dancing, everywhere we go
Marry me

Waited all my life for me and you, you and me
Let me tell the world you'll marry me, marry me
Let our hearts beat, beat, beat as one
Marry me
And we'll greet life as one

Show the world happy endings still exist
You and me
From the time we first kissed

With love I live to share with you
My life to give for all of you

Marry me
Please say you'll be my wife

Each day begins and ends with the thought of you
Marry me

IF LOVE IS AS I'VE HEARD

AND NOT THE WAY I'VE DREAMED,

I DON'T WANT TO HEAR

THOSE WHO HAVE NOT SEEN

ONE'S OPEN ARMS.

Although we've been friends
Since we were children at play
It seems like we're meeting
For the very first time today

It's not like before
Then it was a breeze.
Now my heart's on the floor
And I feel my shaking knees

Take my hand
It's not just you
I understand

It was so easy yesterday
When all we did was play.
We didn't have to think
Of what to say or not to say

I feel something new
I can't touch or see.
Now there is you
Where there used to be just me.

MAYBE I SHOULD HAVE SAID "HELLO"
OR MAYBE ASKED HER NAME
BUT I DIDN'T
AND EVERY THING STAYED THE SAME

I hear our song
And think of you
Till another song plays
And I'm with someone new

There's always been a song
That went wrong and skipped a beat
Never lasting very long
With anyone that I would meet

I see a smile
And think of you
But it's someone else's smile
I can't remember who

There's always been a smile
For a while, for a time
Still I'm in denial
With everyone I leave behind

I feel your touch
With someone who
May be trying too hard
To take my mind off you

There's always been a face
To replace the one before
To fill an empty space
With anyone outside my door

When will the smiles last
When will the past be past
When will the music last for me

We'll always share
Our cotton candy world out there
Our never ending carousel of dreams

The laughter with the clowns we've seen
Will live as long as we can dream.
When things don't seem to go our way
We'll pull out times from yesterday

Hear the music play
And we're a candy kiss away
From riding rainbows in the sky
Over happiness on display

The ups and downs and turnarounds
Fun house, balloons and popcorn sounds
Will live as long as we can say
They can't take memories away.

Goodbye – won't stop me from loving you
We're only a memory away

W

We don't need a Valentine
A Birthday wish
A Xmas gift
A Holiday card that says your mine

Every Day's a Holiday
Like sweet red wine
We drink each day
With love that stands the test of time

We're fireworks on display
A shooting star
Through the Milky Way
Where every day's a Holiday

Today was like yesterday
And tomorrow will be just like today
A Holiday

I remember my first love

We never kissed or even held hands.

I played baseball most of the time

And watched her walk by with her friends

And wave.

Maybe she wasn't waving to me.

I don't play baseball anymore

And she doesn't wave.

I guess I loved like that a lot

And recovered many times

From my initials being kicked away

By drifting sands.

Where are all my Xmas wishes
Winter walks and chapped lip kisses
What kind of Xmas is this
When love from cupid's arrow misses

My dreams are melting with the snow
And Xmas carols fade with the winter
winds that blow
If this is Xmas – I wouldn't know
If there was a Xmas – where did it go

All I can do is wait till next year
Light the tree and wait for you here
Keep your unwrapped Xmas gifts near
Our Xmas tree the one from last year

Let's be children again!
Let's show everyone when,
We jumped over cracks,
Not to break our mother's backs

We'll show everyone how,
We Save Three Little Pigs somehow
We'll huff and we'll puff,
Till the tough wolf had enough.

I'll be the tortoise, you be the hare.
When you arrive, I will be there.
Please just don't be upset
If you find a marionette.

Is Mary Poppins really you,
Flying around with an extra shoe
Belonging to Cinderella
Trading for her lost umbrella.

Let's be children again!

It's easy to wish, and to dream.
The rainbow's our road to everything.
Come along with us and be,
Anything you want to be.

You'll be Snow White for me
I'll be Bashful, Happy,
Dopey, Sneezy and Doc,
Sleepy, Grumpy, the whole flock.

We will walk hand in hand
Pretending in our wonderland
Pick cookies off a roof,
Disappear by going poof.

Let's be children again!
Let's be children again!

I go on my way

I party and I play

I wrap today around me

But you're still in my way.

Tangled in my sheets

With no other feet but mine

I dream of you and sleep

With memories of mine.

N

othing here looks the same
Our initials in the sand are gone
No sea shells calling out your name
Waves playing someone else's song

Where are the stars we wished upon
Kisses that went on and on
Love we shared from dark till dawn
Is everything once ours, now gone

Send me a sign

Lovers walking hand in hand
In our footsteps that we made
Building castles in the sand
Where we once loved-once played

Do I hear the wind telling me
That now's the time for breaking free
Or are we sharing space in time
Together – you and me

Send me a sign

I called him Uncle
He wasn't, you know
But he'll always walk beside me
Wherever I go.

He held his hand out to me
When I was learning to walk
Because of him, I'm running now
But with my sons I stop to talk.

I'll treasure that special day
He took time to share
His stories filled with warmth
And years of wisdom I could wear.

A stranger wasn't treated
Any different than a brother
His last words to me were
"We have to help each other".

I'll remember those last words
And whenever I can be
A helping hand to others
It will be as Uncle was to me.

ONLY INNOCENCE UNDERSTANDS
WHAT HAPPINESS COMES FROM HOLDING HANDS
AND WANTING MORE AS WE EXPLORE
FEELINGS WE NEVER FELT BEFORE

The bench is empty where we used to sit
And feed the birds that we're no longer with

The still waters mirror the clouds above
Floating away with memories of

You

The squirrels still run around our tree

Where we carved two hearts for the world to see

Like the branches reaching for the sky
I reach out my arms and wonder why

You

I've been here before
Alone with me wanting more
Alone with one wish
And one dream to be more than this

I just have to stay
And find out why
I'm in the here and now
And have to try
To stand tall and win it all
And not say goodbye

Not yet
Till I get
What I came here for

And I will

I feel I can make it
If I can see it, I can take it

There must be a way
To keep my dream from fading away
To open that door
For me to walk through and soar

And I will

Once I Thought I Knew You Well
Never Thought We'd Ever Be This Way.
Who would Believe We Ever Blushed.
Who would Ever Think We'd Say Those Things So Often Hushed.

Once I Thought I Knew You Well.
Now I'm Not So Sure You're The One.
Who Would Ever Think I'd Stop
And Never Give To You Again.

When Did It Happen
Where Was The Gap In
What We Thought Was Love
Maybe It Wasn't In The Cards For Us

Once I Thought I Knew You Well
Once There Wasn't Someone Else's Love
Who would Believe I'd Ever Stop
And Never Feel For You Again.

Once There Were Two Children So In Love
Who would Believe They'd Grow To See
That Children Just Pretend
And They Could Never Be Again.

I know, you know

This isn't pretend for us

We chose, left those

And love became a friend to us

I know, you know

We wanted to run away

Time froze, heat rose

Our bodies became one today

Life slows, love grows

This isn't pretend today

It's nice out today

As the breeze tickles your nose

And you sneeze the truth as it goes on by.

A trickle of a tear

Shows you're not fickle being here today.

You made the darkness disappear

And the rain jump back into the clouds.

I know this is love,

For everything is in its place

And nothing shows in your face

But me.

What are you doing
These days without me - alone
Are you remembering
As I'm remembering – alone

And when you're in our bed
Do you call out for me
If only in your dreams

Come back to me

Time goes so slowly
These days without you – at home
Are you pretending
As I'm pretending – alone

And when the kids cry out
For dad to hold them tight
Do you whisper to yourself

Come back to me

I used to laugh, now I just cry
And let the memories unwind
I close my eyes and just pretend
That I'm still yours and you're still mine

I want to live – I want to feel
All that time forgot to bring
I want your love – I want to feel
The season change to spring

I love you
These days without you – alone
And I'll keep dreaming
That you're dreaming – alone

And when you reach for me
I'll be reaching out for you
If only in a dream

Come back to me

Miss those days
Special days

Just we two!
There isn't anything we two can't do.
Though I may have to change my point of view,
Just for you,
Dreams really can come true

Find a star!
However far, no matter where we are,
Let's wish our dreams,
And they are not that far
From our star.
Wishes are what we are.

Before we met,
Miracles for us were only dreams.
And now it seems,
Our eyes can mesmerize.

Just we two!
Can open up our hearts and listen too,
The ones we left behind and never knew.
Me and you,
It's not too late to do.

In our land!
We can build a castle out of sand.
Have sea shells splash into a marching band
In our land
Where we just waive our hand.

Before our eyes,
Magical is what we want to be
Eternally,
There's nothing we can't do.

Just we two!
Can change our ways and we can start anew.
Just believe in everything we do.
Me and you,
Everything can come true.

Hum a tune!
And everyone is on a honeymoon,
And flying magic carpets to the moon.
To our tune,
There's nothing we can't do.

Just we two!
Me and you.
Just we two!

What does that mean

We'll be in touch
Did they like me a lot
Or not to much

I think they liked me
Didn't they
If they didn't
Wouldn't they say

Why wouldn't they like me
Anyway

Are they just hesitating, waiting,
Debating whether to call
While my heart's pulsating
For maybe nothing at all: .

What does that mean
We'll be in touch
Did they like me a lot
Or not to much

I sang my heart out
Didn't I
From the start out
Exemplify

Why wouldn't they like me
Tell me why

I was at my best
Wasn't I
Best of the rest
In my mind's eye

What does that mean
We'll be in touch

I jumped out of bed
Running room to room
Listening for voices
Gone too soon

Silence grew louder
With each thought of you
My children's noises
Were gone too

If ever I needed
"I love you" repeated
Over and over again

Now is that moment.
If ever I needed "I love you"
Repeated again.

Why was I gone
When you needed me near?
Funny that I can't remember
Leaving here.

I had it all.
But I never knew
How much I have missed.
Now I do.

Knowing's the easy part

Talking about it's not.

Why was tomorrow somehow always missed
For me and you.
How many never do what they plan to do
But come tomorrow they're gonna try
Like me and you

Will we ever catch up with tomorrow

Don't put tomorrow so far down the list.
Like we two.
Don't blink or tomorrow will be gone
And missed for all of you.

Will we ever catch up with tomorrow

When you discover your rainbow of colors
Like we two
Don't let your rainbow fade
Keep them as bright as the stars tonight
For all of you

I remember when
When times were simpler then
When I took time to see
What was in front of me

When times would go sideways
I had to find new ways
To squeeze out time
And make one more dream mine

I always had a dream
A dream to see me through
That yearning part of me
Just wanting to break through

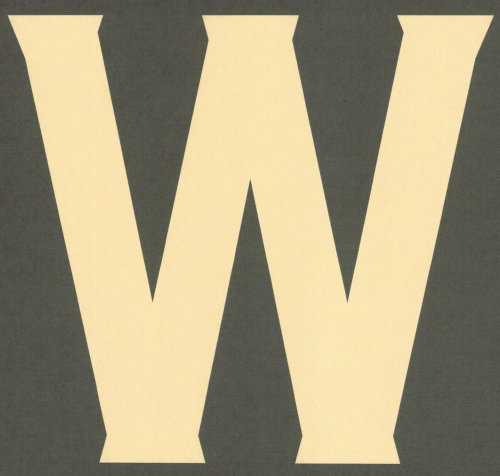

WHY CAN'T I FORGET YOU ALL AT ONCE
CLOSE MY EYES AND JUST SEE ME
WHY CAN'T I FORGET YOU ALL AT ONCE
OPEN MY EYES AND JUST BE FREE

Thank you for that ball
　　　So hard to catch at first
And for no allowance each week.

Thank you for that smack
　　　To quench my thirst
And for teaching me when not to speak.

Thank you for saying "no"
　　　When others said "yes"
And for leaving me alone to get burned.

Thank you for more
　　　When I thought it was less
And for teaching me respect is earned.

Thank you for a mother
　　　Who says yes to me
And a warmth for life that's rare.

Thank you for giving me
　　　Someone to see
Not just to live, but to share.

Thank you for taking part in the right and wrong
　　　And for your non-smiling smile when you knew.

Thank you for teaching me it would be long
　　　Till I see my sons see me, as I see you.

The first cry of our baby
Maybe the sound most sincere
That we will ever hear
Shared year after year

The first cry is tomorrow's
Sorrows, joys and memories
Life's first gentle breeze
One voice rising free

I know the first time we hold you,
Unfold you, with all our being
We'll hear angels sing
Life around us coloring

Your smile will be like ours
The kind people like to see
A small part of us
As you root into a tree

Your first step will get longer
And stronger with every year
And when we're not here
You will persevere

Your life will be the happiest
With the best still yet to come
Life's phenomenon
When two become one

Your love will last forever
Miracles will be shared
And your souls will be bared
In ways never dared

The first cry shared with your son
Is what you'll remember too
Our miracle – now your miracle
With love will see you through

The first words he's yet to form
Will warm each and every day
But, first he'll cry
To let you know he's here to stay

Life's first gentle breeze

"Feelings" Share Them!

THANK YOU!

We hope you enjoyed this walk thru life as much
as we enjoyed bringing it to you.

See you next time!
Larry and Elwyn

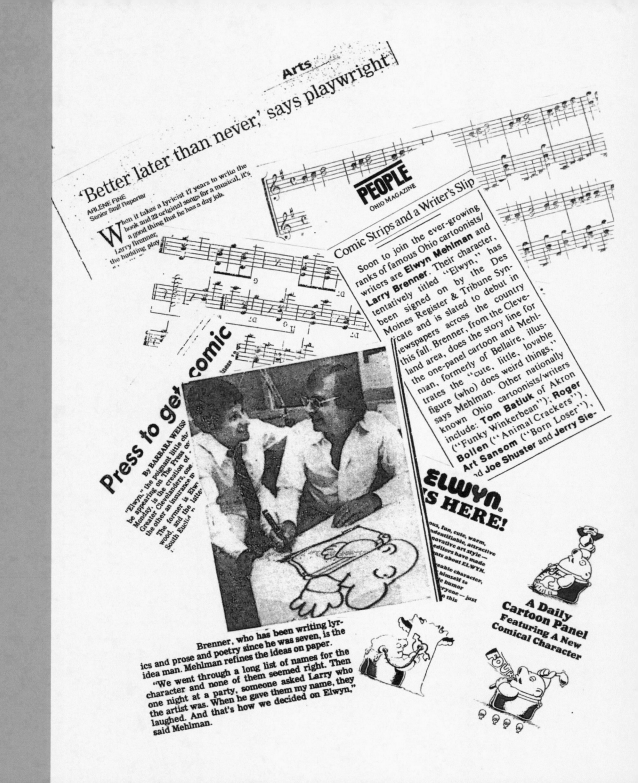

'Better later than never,' says playwright

ARLENE FINE
Senior Staff Reporter

When it takes a lyricist 17 years to write the book and 22 original songs for a musical, it's a good thing that he has a day job.

Larry Brenner, the budding play...

PEOPLE
OHIO MAGAZINE

Comic Strips and a Writer's Slip

Soon to join the ever-growing ranks of famous Ohio cartoonists/writers are **Elwyn Mehlman** and **Larry Brenner**. Their character, tentatively titled "Elwyn," has been signed on by the Des Moines Register & Tribune Syndicate and is slated to debut in newspapers across the country this fall. Brenner, from the Cleveland area, does the story line for the one-panel cartoon and Mehlman, formerly of Bellaire, illustrates the "cute, little, lovable figure (who) does weird things," says Mehlman. Other nationally known Ohio cartoonists/writers include: **Tom Batiuk** of Akron ("Funky Winkerbean"); **Roger Bollen** ("Animal Crackers"), **Art Sansom** ("Born Loser"), and **Joe Shuster** and **Jerry Sie-**

Press to get comic

By BARBARA WEISS

"Elwyn," the poignant little character, be appearing on The Press ca... Monday, is the creation of ... Greater Clevelanders, one ... the other an insurance m... The former is Elw... wood, and the latter... South Euclid ...

ELWYN
IS HERE!

...ous, fun, cute, warm, ...dentifiable, attractive ...novative art style — ...editors have made ...nts about ELWYN.

...eable character, ...himself to ...e humor ...ryone — just ...n this

A Daily
Cartoon Panel
Featuring A New
Comical Character

FOUR

Brenner, who has been writing lyrics and prose and poetry since he was seven, is the idea man. Mehlman refines the ideas on paper.

"We went through a long list of names for the character and none of them seemed right. Then one night at a party, someone asked Larry who the artist was. When he gave them my name, they laughed. And that's how we decided on Elwyn," said Mehlman.

A poem should read

As easy as the air we breathe

Without having to look inside

Around, or underneath

Like the love we share...

We breathe

Feelings   Written by: Lawrence Brenner | Illustrations By: Elwyn Mehlman

Printed in the United States
By Bookmasters